DEBUNKING EVOLUTION: WHAT EVERY CHRISTIAN STUDENT SHOULD KNOW

STUDENT GUIDE

A Six-lesson Video-based Program for Christian Students

Daniel A. Biddle, Ph.D. (editor)

Copyright © 2016 by Genesis Apologetics, Inc.
E-mail: staff@genesisapologetics.com

GENESIS apologetics

http://www.genesisapologetics.com: A 501(c)(3) ministry equipping youth pastors, parents, and students with Biblical answers for evolutionary teaching in public schools.

Prepared by Pat & Sandy Roy, edited by Daniel A. Biddle, Ph.D.

DEBUNKING EVOLUTION: WHAT EVERY CHRISTIAN STUDENT SHOULD KNOW (STUDENT GUIDE)
A Six-lesson Video-based Program for Christian Students
by Daniel A. Biddle, Ph.D. (editor)

Printed in the United States of America

ISBN-13: 978-1533066923

ISBN-10: 1533066922

Reference citations for the sources used in this *Student Guide* can be found in the *Debunking Evolution: What Every Christian Student Should Know* book by the same author.

Unless otherwise indicated, Bible quotations are taken from the HOLY BIBLE, NEW KING JAMES VERSION

Dedication

To my wife, Jenny, who supports me in this work. To my children Makaela, Alyssa, Matthew, and Amanda, and to your children and your children's children for a hundred generations—this book is for all of you. To Dave Bisbee and Mark Johnston, who planted the seeds and the passion for this work.

We would like to acknowledge Answers in Genesis (*www.answersingenesis.org*), the Institute for Creation Research (*www.icr.org*), and Creation Ministries International (*www.creation.com*). Much of the content herein has been drawn from (and is meant to be in alignment with) these Biblical Creation ministries.

Guard what has been entrusted to you, avoiding worldly and empty chatter and the opposing arguments of what is falsely called "knowledge"—which some have professed and thus gone astray from the faith. Grace be with you.
—1 Timothy 6:20–21

"This is the Lord's doing; it is marvelous in our eyes."
— Psalm 118:23

Contents

.

About the Authors

David V. Bassett, M.S. earned his Bachelor of Science in Geology at the University of Texas in El Paso and a Master's of Science in Geological Science from Columbia Pacific University, maintaining a 4.0 post-graduate academic record. He is a high school science teacher with over 28 years' experience in Christian education and has been the Science Department Head of Ovilla Christian School in Ovilla, TX since March 1996. Since then, he has been at the Creation Evidence Museum, located on the bank of the Paluxy River in Glen Rose, Texas, where he has served as the Assistant to the Director, Dr. Carl E. Baugh. Mr. Bassett is a voting member of the Creation Research Society and is the current president of the Metroplex Institute of Origin Science for the Dallas-Ft. Worth area.

Dr. Jerry Bergman has five Master's degrees in the science, health, psychology, and biology fields, a Ph.D. in human biology from Columbia Pacific University, and a Ph.D. in measurement and evaluation from Wayne State University. Jerry has taught biology, genetics, chemistry, biochemistry, anthropology, geology, and microbiology at Northwest State Community College in Archbold Ohio for over 30 years. He is currently an Adjunct Associate Professor at the University of Toledo Medical School. He has over 1,000 publications in 12 languages and 32 books and monographs, including *Vestigial Organs Are Fully Functional*; *Slaughter of the Dissidents: The Shocking Truth About Killing the Careers of Darwin Doubters; The Dark Side of Darwin*; *Hitler and the Nazis Darwinian Worldview: How the Nazis Eugenic Crusade for a Superior Race Caused the Greatest Holocaust in World History and The Darwin Effect. Its influence on Nazism, Eugenics, Racism, Communism, Capitalism & Sexism*. Professor Bergman has also taught at the Medical College of Ohio as a research associate in the Department of Experimental Pathology, at the University of

Toledo, and at Bowling Green State University. Jerry is also a member of MENSA, a Fellow of the American Scientific Association, a member of The National Association for the Advancement of Science, and member of many other professional associations. He is listed in Who's Who in America, Who's Who in the Midwest and in Who's Who in Science and Religion.

Dr. Daniel A. Biddle is president of Genesis Apologetics, Inc. a 501(c)(3) organization dedicated to equipping youth pastors, parents, and students with Biblical answers for evolutionary teaching in public schools. Daniel has trained thousands of students in Biblical Creation and evolution and is the author of several Creation-related publications. Daniel has a Ph.D. in Organizational Psychology from Alliant University in San Francisco, California, an M.A. in Organizational Psychology from Alliant, and a B.S. in Organizational Behavior from the University of San Francisco. Daniel has worked as an expert consultant and/or witness in over 100 state and federal cases in the areas of research methodologies and statistical analysis. Daniel's ministry experience includes over two decades of Church service and completing graduate work at Western Seminary.

David A. Bisbee is the Vice President of Genesis Apologetics, Inc., a non-profit 501(c)(3) organization that equips Christian students attending public schools and their parents with faith-building materials that reaffirm a Biblical Creation worldview. Genesis Apologetics is committed to providing Christian families with Biblically- and scientifically-based answers to the evolutionary theory that students are taught in and public schools. Mr. Bisbee's professional experience includes over 25 years in the field of energy efficiency. For the last 14 years, he has been in charge of a research program which tests energy efficiency technologies in real-world environments. Mr. Bisbee has presented the results of these projects through numerous published reports and educational seminars throughout the

10

United States. Dave's ministry experience includes over 10 years teaching Sunday school classes and creation science presentations.

Caleb LePore is a Research Associate for Genesis Apologetics, Inc., a 501(c)(3) organization dedicated to equipping youth pastors, parents, and students with Biblical answers for evolutionary teaching in public schools. Inspired by the power of the creation message to change his life and the lives of others, Caleb started a creation ministry of his own as a teenager. Now on Genesis Apologetics team, Caleb loves the opportunities to spread the message of the Creator as a speaker and writer. Caleb writes regular articles for the Genesis Apologetics blog, which cover an assortment of creation vs. evolution topics. Caleb is a homeschool graduate, Eagle Scout, and is currently enrolled as a student of CollegePlus!. Caleb hopes to one day work for one of the main creation ministries in the U.S. as a writer, researcher, and speaker.

Roger Patterson is a writer and editor with Answers in Genesis, one of the largest Creation Ministries in the U.S. Roger earned his B.S. Ed. degree in biology and chemistry from Montana State University-Billings. Before joining Answers in Genesis, he taught high school students for eight years in Wyoming's public school system and assisted the Wyoming Department of Education in developing assessments and standards for use in its schools. For many years, he taught from an evolutionary perspective in his classroom until God opened his eyes to the truth of Scripture.

Pat and Sandy Roy are the creators of the audio series *Jonathan Park*, *The Journey to Novarupta*, and *Time Chroniclers*. These programs are entertaining while teaching creation apologetics to children. They have written hundreds of scripts, articles, and books and taught classes on science from a creation standpoint, for the lay person. Pat worked for 12 years at the Institute for Creation Research as the Director of

Broadcast Media. During that time he and his team interviewed hundreds of the top scientists in the Christian community about their findings on creation, and made them understandable to the lay person in the programs *Back to Genesis*, and *Science Scripture Salvation*. These programs aired on radio outlets internationally. Pat has also been a creation speaker for over 25 years.

Dr. Jonathan D. Sarfati has a B.Sc. (Hons.) in Chemistry and a Ph.D. in Spectroscopy (Physical Chemistry). Dr. Sarfati is a research scientist and editorial consultant for Creation Ministries International (CMI) in Brisbane. In this capacity, he is co-editor of Creation magazine, and also writes and reviews articles for *Journal of Creation*, CMI's in-depth, peer-reviewed publication, as well as contributing to CMI's website, *www.creation.com*. Dr. Sarfati has authored or co-authored several notable books, including *Refuting Evolution* (now over 500,000 copies in print), *The Creation Answers Book*, *Refuting Evolution 2*, *Refuting Compromise*, *15 Reasons to Take Genesis as History*, *By Design: Evidence for Nature's Intelligent Designer—the God of the Bible*, and *The Greatest Hoax on Earth? Refuting Dawkins on Evolution*.

Roger Sigler, M.A. is a licensed professional geoscientist in the State of Texas. His diverse background in geology spans oil and gas exploration, core analysis, geothermal systems, groundwater problems, and environmental abatement projects. His latest employment is in core, geological, and drilling fluid analyses at Intertek's Westport Technology Center. He is also a part-time geology instructor at Wharton County Junior College. He has taught creation science since 1989, and helped form the Greater Houston Creation Association where he was president from 1997-2001. He acquired a Master's degree in Geology from the Institute for Creation Research in 1998. He has been published in the 1998 and 2003 *Proceedings of the International Conference on Creationism* and co-authored a poster session on catastrophic debris flows at the 2011 Geological Society of

America. He is a member of the Geological Society of America, Houston Geological Society, American Association of Petroleum Geologists, and Creation Research Society. He is married, has two children, and attends Christ Covenant Church in Houston, Texas.

Dr. Jeffrey Tomkins has a Ph.D. in Genetics from Clemson University, a M.S. from the University of Idaho, and a B.S. from Washington State University. He was on the Faculty in the Department of Genetics and Biochemistry, Clemson University, for a decade, where he published 57 secular research papers in peer-reviewed scientific journals and seven book chapters on genetics, genomics, proteomics, and physiology. For the past several years, Dr. Tomkins has been a Research Scientist at the Institute for Creation Research and an independent investigator publishing ten peer-reviewed creation science journal papers, numerous semi-technical articles, and two books including *The Design and Complexity of the Cell.*

Cornelius Van Wingerden, M.S. taught high school science and math for 21 years. He retired from teaching high school in 2011. Van holds a B.S. in Geology from San Diego State University, an M.S. in Geology from the ICR Graduate School, Santee, California, and a M.A. in Science Education from California State University, Bakersfield. While at ICR, he studied large debris flows found in the Kingston Peak Formation, Death Valley Region.

Overview of the Student Guide

This guide is designed to go hand-in-hand with the *Debunking Evolution: What Every Christian Student Should Know* book and video series (**available at Christian outlets and on our website: *www.debunkevolution.com***).

Lesson One answers the question "Why Is Creation-Evolution Training Important?" We look at the impact that evolution teaching has on today's Christian student and make the case that students should be aware of the typical evolution evidences that are provided in today's schools and Biblical and scientific ways for addressing them.

Lesson Two looks at the assumptions that underlie the "deep time" that evolutionists claim is necessary for evolution theory to work. We contrast the Biblical account where God describes how He spontaneously created all life during Creation Week just thousands of years ago.

Lesson Three takes apart the typical evidences that are used to promote human evolution. The four main icons used in public school are evaluated and contrasted with the Biblical account of human origins. We also take time to debunk the vestigial structures that were supposedly left over from the human and animal evolutionary process.

Lesson Four looks into the primary "mechanisms" that supposedly drive evolution: Adaptation and Natural Selection. We contrast this with the Biblical perspective, which is simply that God pre-programmed genetic variety and adaptability within the blueprint of each animal "kind."

Lesson Five takes a deeper look into evolution theory by exploring Common Ancestors/Branching and Homology, which are two theoretical ways that evolution is supported in textbooks.

Lesson Six looks at some advanced topics that are typically included in most biology textbooks: Fossils, Whale Evolution, and Extinction. These topics are also explored from a Biblical perspective based on Noah's Flood.

Introduction

This Student Guide is designed to be used with our *Debunking Evolution: What Every Christian Student Should Know* book and videos (**available on our website: *www.debunkevolution.com***), which includes 12 videos to prepare students for evolution teaching in public schools, public museums, state parks, etc. This set makes a six-lesson program that can be adapted for students between junior high and college, and facilitated by parents or youth leaders. Our program is based on a straight-forward view on Genesis, and is drawn from research conducted by leading Biblical Creation ministries.

Christians will find this useful for public school students who are confronted with (in some states), over 250 pages of evolution teaching. Homeschool parents will also find it useful for equipping students before going to college. Youth directors and pastors can use this program for Sunday School or small group studies. A student who completes all six lessons will develop an in-depth understanding of the important differences between evolution and creation, and why the Creation account in Genesis can be trusted. The program can also serve as an in-depth study for adults.

Guidance for Facilitators

Each lesson is designed to teach the scientific and Biblical case for Creation and allow students to apply what they've learned at the conclusion of each. This Guide is divided into modules for each of the six weeks. The modules consist of:

 Watch the Video

If you purchased the DVD, selecting the menu item for each lesson will play the videos in each. The videos can also be viewed online at: ***www.debunkevolution.com***.

Each lesson begins by watching 1–3 short videos. They are designed to present the topic in a creative way to hold attention. The videos follow John and Jane through interesting situations as they study for class. John and Jane often quote from the actual textbooks being used in public school. While textbooks vary between states and schools, the concepts covered will likely be very similar. We zoom-in on the charts, graphs, and illustrations so students will identify with the topics being reviewed.

 Fill-in-the Blanks

This section is provided so students can fill-in the blanks as they watch the videos. If students are completing this program as a group, consider offering a reward to those who complete all the fill-ins for that lesson. *Note that the answers are provided in the endnotes at the end of this book.*

 Summary

The summaries cover the scientific case presented in each video. There are a few ways to use this summary:

1. To reinforce what was just taught in the video.

2. Facilitators can read the summary ahead of time to prepare for what will be presented in the video.
3. Students can use this section as a way to review the topic.

 Biblical Discussion

This section goes deeper into the verses covered in the videos. It asks students to apply Biblical thinking to each topic. For a group setting, this will facilitate interesting discussions.

Application

Each lesson ends with a set of questions to solidify what's been covered apply it personally. In a group, these questions are designed to inspire interesting discussions.

Real-life Examples

Each lesson also contains side-bars to demonstrate the topics in real-life examples. These relate to real life, and present interesting insights.

Getting Started

Again, feel free to pick and choose how these modules fit your program. Our prayer is that the *Debunking Evolution Series* will equip your student(s) to know the Biblical and scientific case against evolution, and the overwhelming support for Biblical Creation! May the Lord bless you as you embark on this exciting journey.

Lesson 1: Why Is Creation-Evolution Training Important?

 Watch the Video: *Why Creation?*

> Videos available online: ***www.debunkevolution.com***

 Fill-in-the Blanks: *Why Creation?*

Use the section below to fill in the blanks while watching the video:

Evolution: I am Evolution. I am _____ [1]
_____ [2] accidents.

Creation: I am Creation. I point to the
_____ [3].

Evolution: I had to break a few scientific laws to get here. The Law of Conservation of Mass/Energy which says new matter or energy can never be
_____ [4] nor _____ [5].

Evolution: The Law of Causality, which says that every effect has an equal or greater _____ [6].

Evolution: The Law of Biogenesis says that life always comes from _____ [7].

Creation: My book (the Bible) has stood the test of time. Like the God that revealed it, my truth never
_____ [8].

Creation: His ways are far beyond _____ [9] ways.

Evolution: I am millions of years of _____ [10].

These numbers match the answer key in back!

18

Creation: I, the Creation, groan in pain because of
_____[11] and death. But death was the
_____[12] for the wrongs we commit, not a way
to advance the world.

Evolution: When you die, there will be no reason for
your _____[13] _____[14].

Creation: Believe in God and you will find
_____[15] _____[16].

 Summary: *Why Creation?*

Some people try to combine evolution and creation.
However, these two worldviews are incompatible!

Evolution	Creation
Nothing created everything.	Everything came from a Creator.
Breaks many scientific laws.	Obeys the laws created by God.
Did not leave behind evidence.	Recorded in the Bible.
Theories change.	Account has remained unchanged.
Popular to believe.	The narrow path.
We are our own gods.	We're made by God.
Says life has no value.	We're made in God's image.
Built on millions of years of horrible death.	Made by the living God who says, death will someday be conquered.
No real reason for existence.	Ultimate purpose for living.
Leads to death.	Leads to life.

Biblical Discussion: *Why Creation?*

Read Deuteronomy 30:19:

I call heaven and earth as witnesses today against you, that I have set before you life and death, blessing and cursing; therefore, choose life, that both you and your descendants may live.

1. What does it mean that heaven and earth are witnesses? [17]

2. How does this relate to what we read in Romans 1:18-23? [18]

3. Why do many call evolution the "religion of death"? [19]

4. According to the Bible, why does death exist? (Romans 6:23, 1 Corinthians 15:55-57) [20]

5. What "blessings" will someone receive for trusting the Creation account? [21]

6. What "cursings" come as a result of following evolution? [22]

7. How does someone "choose life"? [23]

Application: *Why Creation?*

Our belief about where we come from will dramatically affect how we live our lives!

1. How will someone live if they truly believe they are molecules that came about by random chance? [24]

Denying the Faith

Does your understanding of the creation account really affect your faith? Charles Templeton was an evangelist heard by thousands in the 1930s and 1940s; later he denied his faith! What caused this change of heart? Here is a letter he sent to his friend Billy Graham:

"Billy, it's simply not possible any longer to believe the biblical account of creation. The world was not created over a period of days a few thousand years ago; it has evolved over millions of years. It's not a matter of speculation; it's a demonstrable fact."

2. How would someone live if they truly understand they were made with ultimate purpose by a God who loves them? [25]

3. What happens to a person who tries to combine these two opposite worldviews? (James 1:5-8) [26]

4. How confident are you about the Creation account found in the Bible? [27]

5. 1 Peter 3:15 says, "Always be ready to give a defense to everyone who asks you a reason for the hope that is in you, with meekness and fear…" How equipped do you feel to share the truth of God's Word with others? [28]

6. What do you need to do to become better equipped? [29]

Lesson 2: Bible History: Real or Fiction?

 Watch the Video: *Radiometric Dating*

Videos available online: *www.debunkevolution.com*

 Fill-in-the Blanks: *Radiometric Dating*

Use the section below to fill in the blanks while watching the video:

John (reading from textbook): If that had happened, Darwin's ideas would have been _____ [30] and _____ [31].

See the back for answers!

John: It sure seems that they're putting their faith in something that they cannot see through direct _____ [32].

John: Actually, the age of the earth is based on the dating of certain _____ [33].

John: Rocks contain radioactive material called the _____ [34] element, or isotope.

John: But, the age is an _____ [35] of those measurements, not an observation.

John: What if the rock already had a _____ [36] isotope in it from the very beginning?

John: Or what if the rock gets _____ [37]?

John: What if the rate of decay was _____ [38] at some point in the past?

John: What was the original ratio of parent to daughter
_____ [39]?

John: One must assume no parent or daughter material was added or _____ [40] from the rock, and that the rate of decay has always been _____ [41] over millions and millions of years.

John: A lava flow in a volcano of the North Island of New Zealand that happened in _____ [42] was dated to be 3.5 million years old.

John: A volcanic bomb that blew out of Mount Stromboli in Italy in _____ [43] was dated to 2.4 million years old.

John: A _____ [44] year old rock from Mount Saint Helen's lava dome dated to 350,000 years – and older.

Jane: How can a rock be _____ [45] million years old, if it holds a fossil of only 36,000 years using a different method?

John: Radiocarbon decays quickly. It has a half-life of only about 5,730 years. So its maximum shelf-life is only about 100,000 years before it becomes _____ [46].

 Summary: *Radiometric Dating*

The genealogies listed in the first eleven chapters of Genesis point back to the first man, Adam, who was created at the end of a six-day creation week about 6,000 years ago. God's description of the creation week in Exodus 20:11 clearly indicates that He *wants us to believe* that creation was only a six-day process: "For in six days the Lord made heaven and earth, the sea, and all that in them is…"

Evolutionary textbooks, however, state that the earth is billions of years old, and that evolution took millions and millions of years to eventually produce the life we see on earth today. If the earth is young, then Darwin's idea would be refuted and abandoned.[a] But are they correct, does science prove the earth to be old?

Radiometric dating relies on observing how quickly radioactive material decays into non-radio-active material. However, dating relies on several unproven assumptions:

1. That scientists knew how much radioactive material was in the rock when it was first formed.
2. That the rock was not contaminated with either the radio-active material, or the material it decays into, from outside the rock.
3. That the rate of decay was constant.

From observation, we know these assumptions must be wrong because several rocks that we know to be young have been dated to be very ancient. So if the dating methods have failed on rocks with known ages, why do we trust them for dating rocks of unknown ages?

[a] Miller, Kenneth R. and Levine, Joseph S. *Biology*. Boston, MA: Pearson, 2006, p. 466.

Novarupta
Novarupta is a volcano in Katmai Park located in the Alaskan Peninsula. It erupted on June 6, 1912. One hundred years later, Dr. David Shormann retrieved a rock sample from the lava dome and had it dated at a professional lab. Although the rock was exactly 100 years old, radiometric dating placed it at 5.5 million years!

Also, radiocarbon decays very quickly—and wouldn't even be detectable after 100,000 years; and yet, we still find them in diamonds that are supposedly billions of years old. A better explanation is that diamonds are much younger.

The evidence shows that radiometric dating does not work, and things are actually much younger than claimed. This is a serious problem for the foundation of evolution, which depends on "deep time." Instead, the evidence fits with the thousands of years of earth history recorded in the Bible!

 Watch the Video: *Uniformitarianism*

Videos available online: *www.debunkevolution.com*

 Fill-in-the Blanks: *Uniformitarianism*

Use the section below to fill in the blanks as you watch the video:

Jane: Right here, they believe all the continents were together to form _____ [47] 225 million years ago.

Jane: Thousands of scientists believe in fast _____ [48] _____ [49], rather than slow continental drift.

Jane (reading from textbook): Geologists make inferences based on the principle of uniformitarianism. This principle states that the same processes that operate today operated in the _____ [50].

Jane: But what this principle refuses to take into account is the major _____ [51] events of the past.

Jane: During the 1980s eruptions of Mount Saint Helens, _____ [52] layers of rock were deposited in three hours.

Jane: The rocks didn't shatter like they should have. They must have bent together while they were soft and _____ [53].

Jane: If the river slowly carved the canyon, then we should see all the material piled up in a river delta, but it's completely _____ [54].

Jane: Animals have to be quickly buried in sediment so its cells can be preserved and then replaced by the surrounding _____ [55].

Jane: And they found many dinosaur bones with red blood cells, soft tissue, proteins, and even _____ [56].

John: Noah's Flood would create many of the rock layers that stretch over entire continents, and bury millions of creatures for us to find as _____ [57] today.

Summary: *Uniformitarianism*

Most secular scientists believe the continents were together in a super continent, called Pangea, about 225 million years ago. Dr. John Baumgardner invented the software, TERRA, which models the movements of the earth. He, and many other creation scientists have demonstrated that the continents "sprint" (rather than drifted) apart—breaking up Pangea very rapidly, instead of over millions of years.

The belief that continental drift takes millions of years is an example of *uniformitarian* thinking—that present processes are key to the past. For example, they determine the speed at which a river is cutting through a canyon, and then use that to determine how old it is. However, what uniformitarian thinking does not account for is catastrophic events that were operating much faster in the past.

During the 1980s eruptions at Mount Saint Helens, 200 layers of rock were deposited in three hours and entire canyon systems were carved in months—some through 700 feet of hard rock!

What happened at Mount Saint Helens causes us to think about places like Grand Canyon. Were those layers laid down quickly? Could the canyon have been rapidly eroded? The evidence seems to support this idea. If the layers of the canyon had been deposited over a very long time, they should be brittle, and would snap when bent. Yet, the layers of the canyon are found bent, all together, demonstrating they were soft and pliable at the same time. Also, if the river slowly carved the canyon, there should be 1,000 cubic miles of material in the river delta below, but it's all missing. It appears to have been swept away by a catastrophe.

When an animal dies, it must be buried very rapidly, and in the right conditions for it to fossilize before it has a chance to deteriorate or be eaten. However, all around the world we see millions of fossils that were *instantly* deposited and fossilized. There are clams that were fossilized before they had a chance to open. A fossilized fish was discovered with another fish in its mouth. An Ichthyosaur was even caught giving birth. Dinosaur bones with red blood cells, soft tissue, proteins, and even DNA have also been found. How long could that last? All of this is proof that fossilization happens very quickly.

Krukowski Quarry

At a quarry near Mosinee, Wisconsin, all kinds of fossilized jelly fish have been found. Now think about their soft body. How quickly would one have to be buried and fossilized before it began to deteriorate? This is definitely a testimony to rapid fossilization!

This just shows that Charles Darwin was wrong when he said, "No organism wholly soft can be preserved."

A global flood would kill animals, bury them, and cause rapid fossilization. Many fossils are found in layers that stretch over huge areas; sometimes over an entire continent and onto others. So what many claim takes millions of years of uniformitarian processes, may happen very rapidly with events like the worldwide flood!

 Biblical Discussion: *Radiometric Dating/ Uniformitarianism*

Read Job 38:4:

Where were you when I laid the foundations of the earth? Tell Me, if you have understanding.

1. In the above verse, God is asking Job if he could explain the creation of the world. How does this relate to man's claims that he knows how old the earth is? [58]

2. Why would God ask this question? And what does it tell us about trusting God's Creation account? [59]

Read 2 Peter 3:3-6:

Knowing this first: that scoffers will come in the last days, walking according to their own lusts, and saying, "Where is the promise of His coming? For since the fathers fell asleep, all things continue as they were from the beginning of creation." For this they willfully forget: that by the word of God the heavens were of old, and the earth standing out of water and in the water, by which the world that then existed perished, being flooded with water.

3. Which part of this verse relates to uniformitarian thinking? In what way? [60]

4. What does it mean that, *"by the **word** of God the heavens were of old"*? [61]

5. What did they willfully forget? [62]

6. Is this verse is talking about a local flood? [63]

7. What does this verse call those who deny the worldwide flood? [64]

8. What does, *"For this they willfully forget"* mean? [65]

9. According to the first part of this passage, what else are these scoffers denying? [66]

ⓘ Application: *Radiometric Dating/Uniformitarianism*

The video quoted the textbook passage on what would have happened if the earth was proven to be young, "Darwin's ideas would have been refuted and abandoned." For that reason, the age of the earth is foundational to the creation/evolution debate.

1. Many Christians accept the evolutionary age of the earth, and reject the Biblical genealogies in Genesis that point back to Creation just thousands of years ago. Why do you think that happens? [67]

2. If the age of the earth is based mainly on radiometric dating, and the video presented the case that it doesn't work, can we trust all of the other dates in the geologic column? [68]

3. Can you explain in your own words why uniformitarianism can't explain the ancient ages of things like the formations of canyons, rock formations, or fossilization? [69]

4. Many things considered to be ancient, are actually excellent proof for the worldwide flood. Can you name three presented in the videos? [70]

5. Can you name one way the eruption at Mount Saint Helens demonstrated what might have been happening during the worldwide flood? [71]

6. For Christians that believe the evolutionary ages of the earth, where do they fit those millions of years into the Bible? [72]

7. Many Christians put millions of years of animals living and dying before Adam and Eve had a chance to sin. Why is that a problem? [73]

Lesson 3: Human Evolution: Did Humans Evolve from Ape-like Creatures?

 Watch the Video: *Human Evolution*

Videos available online: *www.debunkevolution.com*

 Fill-in-the Blanks: *Human Evolution*

Use the section below to fill in the blanks while watching the video:

John: Piltdown Man was called the find of the 20th Century. I think it was the New York Times that said that it proves the theory of _____ [74].

John: Then in 1953 they discovered that the skull was a _____ [75].

John: Nebraska Man was the first American ape-man fossil to be discovered. And Harold Cook found just a _____ [76].

John: But ten years later they discovered that tooth was actually from an _____ [77] pig.

John: So Piltdown Man was the popular proof for evolution for _____ [78] years, and Nebraska Man was the popular proof for _____ [79].

John: It looks like today's truth is tomorrow's _____ [80].

Jane: So it looks like *Homo erectus* wasn't becoming human, but was _____ [81] human.

34

John: In fact, some scientists are fighting to have *Homo habilis* _____ [82] as *Australopithecus.*

John: Really, the way it looks, is that Lucy's just an extinct _____ [83].

Jane: That settles it, if they can live together, and if they have children together, then Neanderthals are just _____ [84], but the difference is that their appearance varies.

Jane: So either these fossils are completely human, or completely ape, with nothing _____ [85].

John: All the specimens from all the different ape-men they've actually found–you can fit them in the back of a small _____ [86] _____ [87].

 Summary: *Human Evolution*

Many people are convinced of the evolutionary story by the supposed fossil transition from an ape-like creature to modern humans. But the truth is that ape-man fossils become popular for a season, but then are later discarded for newer discoveries.

For example, Piltdown man was the "undeniable" truth for 40 years, later followed by Nebraska Man which was popular for 10 years. For a half-century, these two fossils convinced many of evolution. However, it finally came out that the Piltdown skull was an outright fraud, and that Nebraska Man was comprised of nothing more than a pig's tooth!

While today's students are told there is an airtight case, the truth is, most textbooks don't even agree on the dates these supposed ape-men lived. And when you compare these textbook dates to the ones assigned when the fossils were originally discovered, the problem gets even worse.

We want to look at four of the ape-man fossils presented in textbooks now. We'll start with humans, then work backwards. The first is *Homo erectus*. Studies have shown that these skulls actually have a variety of shapes and sizes. One study compared modern Aborigines from Australia to *Homo erectus*, and found they shared a majority of traits. So, it appears that *Homo erectus* wasn't becoming human, but already was!

Next back is *Homo habilis*. There is no agreement among scientists on how to really classify these fossils. Some are even fighting to have them re-classified as *Australopithecus*—which is the next fossil back on many charts.

Neanderthals

This picture of a Neanderthal appeared in the Illustrated London News in February of 1909.

Recently, there has been overwhelming evidence that Neanderthals were actually human. How do you think the public was biased when they saw the above illustration? It demonstrates how evolutionists sometimes make an effort to portray human fossils as being ape-like, and ape fossils as being human-like.

The most famous of the *Australopithecines* is Lucy. While she is often shown standing-up, with eye-whites (apes have brown), and looking very human-like, they have only found partial fragments of her skull and skeleton. While many more fossils of *Australopithecines* have been discovered, it has become obvious they are nothing more than an extinct ape.

Another popular fossil is the Neanderthal. When first discovered, they were depicted as brutish ape-men. However, evolutionists now show them to be very human-like, and claim they were just another branch on the evolutionary tree, and very similar to humans. Recent discoveries show that Neanderthals practiced religion, used tools, played musical instruments, made artwork, and even lived with and had families with humans. This evidence shows clearly that they were in fact human, with some physical differences like humans of different regions can even have today.

Textbooks make it seem like the case for evolution is overwhelming. However, many don't realize all the fossils that supposedly prove evolution could fit in the back of one pick-up truck bed! So, while they present the most popular ape-man fossils with confidence today, they will soon be discarded for new ones!

 Watch the Video: *Vestigial Structures*

Videos available online: *www.debunkevolution.com*

 Fill-in-the Blanks: *Vestigial Structures*

Use the section below to fill in the blanks as you watch the video:

John: So they're saying that animals and people have _____[88] in their bodies that once served a function in our evolutionary ancestors?

John: They're saying its ancestor used to walk on land, but once the dolphin evolved to live in water, it has useless left-over _____[89] _____[90].

Jane: Scientists recently discovered that _____ [91] animals, like whales, need these bones during mating season.

Jane: They point out that our coccyx–the tailbone–is left-over from when we had _____ [92].

Jane: Tiny muscles, tendons, and ligaments connect to it, and it supports something called the pelvic diaphragm. This whole system holds a bunch of _____ [93] and organs in place.

Jane: Some studies now show that in some cases removing your tonsils can be _____ [94] in the long run, especially for young children.

Jane: Proteins called antibodies produced by immune cells in the tonsils help kill germs and prevent _____ [95] and lung infection.

Jane: When you fight an intestinal disease your body gets rid of bacteria, both good and bad, but then the appendix can quickly resupply your system with _____ [96] bacteria.

Jane: A German anatomist by the name of Robert Wiedersheim made a list of 86 vestigial structures in the human body. Later, evolutionists expanded the list to about 180; but modern science has now show that every one of them has a _____ [97].

 Summary: *Vestigial Structures*

Many evolutionists believe there are biological structures that once played a role in evolutionary ancestors. They point out that if humans and creatures were specially created they should not have useless organs and structures. Therefore, they claim these structures were simply passed on from our ancestors and no longer serve an important function.

For example, textbooks point to left-over "hip bones" in dolphins. They supposedly demonstrate that, since dolphins don't have hips, they are "hand-me-downs" from their land-dwelling ancestors. However, a new study shows these bones in similar marine animals are actually used as claspers during mating season. So, while textbooks list them as "left-over hip bones," the truth is they actually do serve a purpose, and were not hip bones at all.

Plica semilunaris

Many evolutionists claim this little fold on the edge of your eye is a left-over from a nictitating eyelid like we find in birds, reptiles, and fish. They believe it was passed on from our evolutionary ancestors.

But this important structure isn't a useless hand-me-down at all! It secretes the substance that makes the crust when we wake up in the mornings. That substance coats foreign objects to protect our eye until the tears wash it away. It also protects against infection.

Likewise, some evolutionists point to the human coccyx as a left-over tail. But the coccyx serves an important function. It is the anchor point for many muscles, tendons, and ligaments. The coccyx also supports the pelvic diaphragm.

The tonsils have also been listed as a vestigial structure, but antibodies produced by immune cells in the tonsils help kill germs and help prevent throat and lung infections. They are actually the first line of defense against inhaled or ingested viruses.

Another popular structure to be named vestigial is the appendix. This organ is the storehouse for beneficial bacteria. When fighting an intestinal disease, your body gets rid of both good and bad bacteria. The appendix helps to repopulate the good bacteria. It also plays a role in the immune system. So, while some of these structures can be removed from our bodies, they still have a beneficial role.

In the late 1800s Robert Wiedersheim, a German Anatomist published a list of 86 vestigial structures. Later, evolutionists increased the list to about 180. But modern science has now demonstrated that each one has a purpose. So, instead of being useless left-overs, these structures were actually created with purpose.

 Biblical Discussion: *Human Evolution/Vestigial Structures*

Read 1 Corinthians 15:39:

All flesh is not the same flesh, but there is one kind of flesh of men, another flesh of animals, another of fish, and another of birds.

1. How does this verse differ from the idea that humans evolved from an ape-like ancestor? [98]

2. What does this verse mean for Christians who say God used evolution to create? [99]

Read Psalm 139:14:

I will praise You, for I am fearfully and wonderfully made; Marvelous are Your works, And that my soul knows very well.

3. How does this Bible passage contrast with the idea that random evolution changed an ape-like creature into you? [100]

4. How does this Scripture compare to the evolutionary idea that we are made-up of left-over parts? [101]

5. When this verse states, "fearfully *and* wonderfully made," it is referring to the amazing complexity of human design. Why does this present a problem for evolutionists? [102]

6. How would someone's life change if they went from believing they were made-up of left-over parts from evolutionary ancestors to the truth that they were fearfully and wonderfully made by God, with ultimate purpose? [103]

7. The verse ends with, "…and *that* my soul knows very well," seems to indicate confidence. How does trusting the Bible's account that they were created give someone confidence? [104]

ⓘ Application: *Human Evolution/Vestigial Structures*

The videos presented evidence that humans did not evolve from an ape-like creature. Further, we have been made marvelously by God, not from left-over evolutionary parts.

1. Some Christians try to combine evolution with the Bible. But if humans evolved from ape-like creatures, what does that do to the account of Adam and Eve? [105]

2. Even when presented with facts to show the fossils do not fit the transition from ape-men to people, many will still hold to the evolutionary story. Why is that? [106]

3. The Bible says we are made in God's image. Can the evolutionary story fit with that idea? [107]

4. According to the Bible, what does it mean to be made in God's image? [108]

5. If we are nothing more than highly-evolved animals, what does it mean for morality? [109]

6. What is the result when people are told that they are nothing more than animals made from evolutionary left-overs? [110]

7. How can the information presented in these two videos make you a better witness? [111]

Lesson 4: Creation-Evolution 101: Adaptation & Natural Selection

 Watch the Video: *Adaptation*

Videos available online: ***www.debunkevolution.com***

Fill-in-the Blanks: *Adaptation*

Use the section below to fill in the blanks while watching the video:

Jane: But this isn't evolution by natural forces if these animals were _____ [112] to adapt like that.

John: Our book lists the sources of genetic variation. This page lists the two main sources of change as mutations and genetic _____ [113].

John: Mutations are usually caused when there is an _____ [114] copying a creature's genetic information which is found in its DNA.

John: Mutations might be able to create a new combination of letters, but it needs to have a meaning for a cell to use as a blueprint later on. In other words, a code isn't really a _____ [115] without some assigned meaning.

John: By losing information, they lost control of an enzyme's production. Now evolution needs to explain gains of _____ [116] over time.

John: People count on that loss of information from mutations to create the genetic _____ [117] for every living creature on earth, out of nothing.

John: So God not only created all the animals, He packed them with enough genetic information that would allow them to adapt to different environments and _____ [118] we see today.

John: So a population of animals can adapt by expressing variety over time, but there are _____ [119] to how much they can change.

 Summary: *Adaptation*

Textbooks are full of examples of how creatures change. Finch beaks for example, or the shells of tortoises. Many evolutionists consider any change to be evolution. One textbook made the case that the two main sources of change were *mutations* and *genetic variation.*

Mutations are usually caused when there is a copy error in a creature's genetic information. It can lose or duplicate letters in the genetic code. Some mutations might be able to create new combinations of letters, but they would need to create *meaning* for the cells to have as a blueprint later on. A code isn't a code unless it has some pre-assigned meaning. So mutations are actually a *loss* of information.

Mutations are actually harmful to a creature. In some cases, science textbooks present beneficial mutations. For example, mosquitos becoming less affected by pesticides, bacteria becoming more resistant, bone density, and humans becoming more resistant to HIV. In these cases, it is still a loss of information that resulted in a benefit. But the challenge for evolution is that mutations can only lose information, and yet are believed to create enough information to turn a single cell into a complex human! How much information would that take?

The other main source of change is genetic variation—or adaptation. God not only created the original kinds of animals, but packed them with enough genetic variability that they could adapt to different environments and express variety. However, the change has limitations. Think of a pair of dice. You can roll anything from 2–12. They express variety, but with limits. Likewise, the different animals can also express variety with limits. Think of all the different types of dogs, and yet they are all still dogs. They can never become a different kind of animal.

So when textbooks show differences in finch beaks or tortoise shells, they demonstrate great examples of adaptation and variation,

Galapagos Iguanas

The Galapagos Islands are crawling with marine and land iguanas. The marine iguanas (top) are black and feed on algae under the water. The land iguanas (bottom) are more of a tan color and live out of the water. Yet, we know both are from the same created kind because they can produce offspring.

This is an example in which we see that God not only created a kind, but also packed them with enough genetic variability to adapt to a variety of different environments.

but then the pass it off as evolution. While they can show the changes in a finch beak, they cannot explain where the finch beak came from in the first place. Finches may vary, but they are still just birds!

Watch the Video: *Natural Selection*

Videos available online: ***www.debunkevolution.com***

 Fill-in-the Blanks: *Natural Selection*

Jane (reading from textbook): Natural Selection is the process by which organisms with variations most suited to their local environment _____ [120] and leave more offspring.

John: But rather than this process producing just the varieties we see among animal kinds, they believe this process built those animals from completely different ones, and can eventually lead to one kind of animal turning into another, but this has never been _____ [121].

John: Evolutionists believe that Natural Selection figured out how to design an eye. But how? It would have to build and preserve over, who knows how many generations, hundreds of _____ [122], interacting eye parts.

Jane: You're right. Natural Selection is just a process; it doesn't have a brain. It can't _____ [123] or design.

Jane: It's like they've replaced God's power with _____ [124] mutations and natural selection.

47

John: Mutants are usually worse off since most mutations are harmful. And Natural Selection actually cleanses the population by killing the less _____ [125] mutants.

Jane: So the real world works exactly opposite of what evolution _____ [126].

John: And when you think about it, Natural Selection can't really _____ [127] anything.

John: There's no known mechanism for creating information like we find in DNA, from _____ [128] matter.

John: Evolution claims that a never-ending chain of struggle and _____ [129] is what created life.

 Summary: *Natural Selection*

Natural selection is supposed to be one of the two main processes that makes up evolution. Evolutionists believe a mutation takes place in the genetic code, causing a new trait to be expressed in its offspring. That trait supposedly gives an advantage and natural selection favor the mutants, which soon outnumber the others who eventually die out. Then the scenario repeats with another variation, supposedly driving evolution forward. But is this how things really work?

Textbooks like to point out examples of natural selection, like Polar Bears who have the advantage in the snow because of their white coat, or green grasshoppers that have an advantage over yellow ones when birds are hunting them in a green environment. So how did those changes happen? Did the grasshoppers know how to engineer their color to be more camouflaged? Can a polar bear design its coat to be white?

Evolution actually claims that these changes happened through random mutations–the beneficial were passed along, but the bad ones died out. But think about what they are saying–that animals, which are so complicated that man is still scratching the surface of understanding them—were engineered by random chance. It defies belief to think such amazing engineering was done without intelligence. By doing this, they are assigning natural selection (which doesn't have a brain) god-like powers!

Baraminology

Evolutionists study the evolutionary relationships between *species*. However, Baraminology is the study of the Biblical created *kinds*, and the variety they can express. For example, it's been demonstrated that different species of monkeys come from the same created kind because they can interbreed.

Another problem is that natural selection can only judge based on a creature's overall ability to survive, but the changes actually need to happen deep-down inside the genes. So natural selection is blind to what is happening on the genetic level.

There are even bigger problems for natural selection. For example, if a fish tank was knocked over and only half were put back, was it survival of the fittest? No. It was survival of the luckiest. Or what about two fruit flies, one normal, and the other a mutant with shriveled wings? Which one would most likely survive? Most likely the normal one, leaving the normal population preserved—which is just the opposite of what evolution needs!

So mutations lose information and natural selection can't create anything, it only can deselect by killing whole individuals. How then, could this process turn a single cell into a complex human?

The biggest problem for evolutionists is the origin of life in the first place. No one has answered the question of how non-living material could arrange itself into molecules with information to create the first life. Information always comes from an *intelligent* source.

Finally, evolution says that it was a never-ending chain of struggle and death that created life. But the Bible says that life came from life, and that life was created by God.

 Biblical Discussion: *Adaptation/Natural Selection*

Read Genesis 1:25:

And God made the beast of the earth according to its kind, cattle according to its kind, and everything that creeps on the earth according to its kind. And God saw that it was good.

1. Just considering this verse alone, does it sound like God created each kind of animal fully formed, or could it mean that He used evolution? [130]

2. Count how many times the word "kind" appears in Genesis, chapter 1. Now please review 1 Corinthians 15:39. Then read Genesis 6:20 and 8:18-19. What concept is God communicating in His word? [131]

3. How do you think a Biblical "kind" differs from the concept of a species? [132]

4. It appears God not only created the Biblical kinds, but also packed them with enough genetic variability to adapt to different environments and express variety. What does that tell you about the creativity of Christ, the Creator? [133]

5. What does Genesis 1:25 mean when it states, "*it was good*"? [134]

Read 1 Corinthians 15:55-57

O Death, where is your sting? O Hades, where is your victory?

6. What does this verse mean? [135]

7. Evolution relies on the struggle for survival and death to create life. How does that differ from the Biblical view of death? [136]

❗ Application: *Adaptation/Natural Selection*

The videos demonstrate that there is no real mechanism for evolution. For Christians, that means that we don't have to be intimidated by supposed scientific theories that teach there is no God.

1. Many Christians don't believe the plain meaning of the Creation account because they try to combine it with evolution. But after watching these videos, how would you answer someone who holds that view? [137]

2. People are often confused because they see adaption and variation really happening, and mistake that for evolution of one kind of animal into another. Can you explain the difference between adaptation and variation and the idea that mutations and natural selection can create new basic kinds of animals? [138]

3. The videos presented the idea that natural selection actually works the opposite of what evolution requires. Can you explain why? [139]

4. When Christians come to understand that evolution is not true, their confidence in God's Word becomes stronger, and they begin to live more powerful lives. What about your own faith? How do you find it affected by seeing the scientific case for God's Word? [140]

5. When you realize God not only created the original kinds of animals, but was also creative enough to pack them full of the genetic variability we see expressed in so many wonderful varieties, does it lead you to worship the Creator? In what ways? [141]

6. Contrast the hope offered between these two different ideas: evolution, which says life came from millions of years of survival of the fittest and death; and the Biblical concept that death is an intrusion into Creation and has been conquered by Christ. [142]

7. Most evolutionists cannot explain specifically how evolution works. In this lesson we've described the theory that mutations and natural selection are what supposedly drive evolution forward. If God calls you to witness to an evolutionist, do you feel equipped to explain why evolution doesn't work? If not, what do you need to do to become equipped? [143]

Lesson 5: Creation-Evolution 102: Common Ancestors/Branching & Homologous Structures

 Watch the Video: *Common Ancestors/Branching*

Videos available online: *www.debunkevolution.com*

Fill-in-the Blanks: *Common Ancestors/Branching*

Use the section below to fill in the blanks while watching the video:

John: His (Carl Linnaeus') work was the basis for the
_____ [144] system we still use today.

John: Later, Charles Darwin sketched a diagram to show how life started simple and then
_____ [145] out to every creature on earth.

John: These charts show groups of organisms they believe share a _____ [146] ancestor.

Jane (reading): Remember that cladograms are visual presentations of hypotheses about _____ [147], and not hard and fast facts.

Jane: But these branching points are just imaginary lines that represent the hypotheses about which animals evolved from a common _____ [148].

Jane: From the beginning God created fully formed kinds of animals. So it isn't a tree like _____ [149] thought, instead it's an orchard.

Jane: We see variation happening all the time, but we never see the evolutionary process of
_____[150] and selection creating new kinds.

John: So dogs, apes and people can show variety, but can never _____[151] into a new kind.

Jane: Just think about all the variety in the breeds of dog kind–*Canis familiaris*–in the last _____[152] years.

Jane: What if God made each basic kind with potential to change some of its traits, but no _____[153] to morph into a different kind?

 Summary: *Common Ancestors/Branching*

Carl Linnaeus is credited as being the first to create the system that has become our modern classification for animals. Later, Charles Darwin drew a chart in which he showed simple life branching out to all the different creatures we have nowadays. Thus was born the Evolutionary Tree of Life.

Textbooks are filled with similar charts called *cladograms*. These charts group animals based on supposed shared ancestors. But as the Miller and Levine *Biology* textbook says, "Remember that cladograms are visual presentations of hypotheses about relationships, and not hard and fast facts." That's because they only represent actual animals at the tips of the branches. All the lines connecting their relationships are only theories, not based on actual facts.

While evolutionists have a tree, creationists show it is actually an orchard. God created fully formed animals which have the ability to adapt and express variety, but cannot change into a completely different kind of animal. Like an orchard, there are many different trees, or kinds, animals. Then each of those animals can branch out into different varieties. For instance, we see the dog, ape, and human kinds that express variety, but a dog can never become a monkey, and a monkey cannot become a human. There is only so far that genetic recombination can go.

Walcott Quarry

This quarry is located in the Canadian Rockies of British Columbia. It is a well-known fossil site because evolutionists believe it represents a sudden "explosion" of new varieties of life.

Here are some observations we make at this site:

1. Fully formed creatures.
2. No transitional fossils turning into others.
3. Small variations within the same kind of creature.

Does this evidence better support the idea of the *evolutionary tree* or the *creation orchard*?

Because of their belief that all change is evolution, evolutionists name many of the variations they find in the fossil record (or living creatures) as new species. But often it's just a variation *within the created kind*. Think about a paleontologist from the future digging up the fossils of a Bulldog, a Chihuahua, and a Great Dane. They would surely classify them as different species, but in reality, they are all the same created kind.

As it turns out, the fossil record, animal classification, and the Bible all point back to the concept of original created kinds that can also express variety. It's an orchard, not a tree.

Watch the Video: *Homologous Structures*

Videos available online: *www.debunkevolution.com*

 Fill-in-the Blanks: *Homologous Structures*

John (reading from book): Homologous structures are structures that share a common ancestry. That is, a similar structure in two organisms can be found in the _____[154] ancestor of the organisms.

John: Sometimes we see structures with similar functions in creatures that don't come from a supposed common _____[155].

John: Both humans and squid have a lens that projects an image onto a _____[156].

John: That means a very similar eye had to evolve twice – completely _____[157] of the other.

John: Think about flight. Man with all his intelligence just figured out how to fly less than 200 years ago. But flight supposedly evolved _____[158] different times.

John: When similar structures are found on creatures that aren't considered _____[159] related they are called convergent.

John: When similarities fit evolution they are homologous structures, but when they don't fit, they claim the _____[160] evolved more than once.

Jane: Their evolutionary story decides what is homologous, and they say homologous structures _____[161] evolution.

John: God built similarly designed features into His creatures, making sure that each feature was _____[162] tailored to fit the creature's systems.

John: So similar structures point back to an intelligent and creative God, not to the _____[163] reasoning or random coincidences of evolution.

 Summary: *Homologous Structures*

Sometimes in nature we see animals that have similar structures. These are called *homologous structures*. According to the California *Life Science* textbook, "Homologous structures are structures that share a common ancestry. That is, a similar structure in two organisms can be found in the common ancestor of the organisms."

For example, the theory of evolution holds that penguins, alligators, bats, and humans all evolved from a common ancestor because they have similar bones in their forelimbs. What an impossible job—having to look at the entire animal kingdom and determine which animals evolved from others! Homologous structures are thought to be helpful to arrange animals into evolutionary groupings, but in actuality, they just show how the same Designer used similar features for similar purposes, like mobility.

Relying on homologous structures to try to prove evolution has some serious problems. Sometimes we see a similar structure in two creatures that evolution theory would hold are not closely related at all. Take the case of a human and

58

squid eye. Evolution theory holds that these two different creatures split on the evolutionary tree before their common ancestor had a chance to evolve an eye. To solve the problem, they propose that a similar eye had to evolve twice. This is called *convergent evolution*. Another example is flight. Evolution theory holds that this ability evolved four different times: insects, birds, mammals (like bats), and reptiles (like pterodactyls). The idea that an eye or flight could evolve in the first place is impossible. But now it is four times impossible!

So when two similar structures are similar and thought to come from a common ancestor, they are called *homologous*. When similar structures are found on creatures not thought to be closely related, it is called *convergent*.

This is circular reasoning. When similar structures are supposed to be related they call they them homologous. Then they use those homologous structures to prove evolution. But when they aren't related, they just say it evolved twice and call them convergent.

So how does a Creationist explain similar structures? They simply share a master Designer. Humans make wheels for airplanes, skateboards, cars, and motorcycles. They all look similar, but

Marsupials and Convergent Evolution

Marsupials give birth to babies that continue to develop in the mother's pouch. For that reason, evolutionists say that placental mammals and marsupials are not closely related. Traits that are similar must have evolved separately. As you check out the pictures below, think about the impossibility of random chance creating the same thing twice!

Mammal	Marsupial
Wolf	Tasmanian Tiger
Marmot	Wombat
Anteater	Numbat

are specially designed for a particular vehicle. Likewise, God used similar designs for different creatures, but tailored each for their specific function.

 Biblical Discussion: *Common Ancestors/Branching*

Read Genesis 1:21

> *So God created great sea creatures and every living thing that moves, with which the waters abounded, according to their kind, and every winged bird according to its kind. And God saw that it was good.*

1. The verse says, "…*and every living thing.*" How does that argue against the idea God created a simple lifeform and then guided evolution? [164]

2. How does the idea of a *creation orchard* fit with this verse? [165]

3. What does the first part of the verse mean for those who believe a whale evolved from a wolf-like creature? [166]

4. What does the second part of the verse mean for the idea that birds evolved from dinosaurs? [167]

Read Nehemiah 9:6

You alone are the LORD; You have made heaven, the heaven of heavens, with all their host, the earth and everything on it, the seas and all that is in them, And You preserve them all. The host of heaven worships You.

5. Imagine the power to create the heavens, the heaven of heavens, the earth with everything on it, and the seas and all that is in them. With that in mind, what does this verse mean when it says, "*You alone are the LORD*"? [168]

6. How does the phrase "*You preserve them all*" compare to Colossians 1:17? What does it mean? [169]

7. We read. "*The host of heaven worships You.*" When we investigate the marvels of creation, what should it lead us to do? [170]

! Application: *Common Ancestors/Branching*

In the videos we've learned the difference between the *evolutionary tree* and *creationist's orchard*. Further, we saw how the theory of evolution has serious problems in grouping all of the animals into the evolutionary tree, and that what we find instead is that each kind of creature was created to be its own kind.

1. Can you give a few reasons why the evidence better supports the idea of the *creation orchard* instead of the *evolutionary tree*? [171]

2. Imagine that you had a hundred plastic animals: rodents, chickens, fish, zebras, dinosaurs, blowfish, camels, doves, lizards—and on and on. One hundred! Now pretend you had to line them up in a logical order to tell a story about how one evolved into another. Your line-up can have different branches that split-off, and then split again. Can you picture it? Now imagine the challenges you would face. What specific problems would you encounter? [172]

3. Think about the scenario above. Now imagine the challenge that the theory of evolution has! Some have estimated there are 8.7 million species on earth. Evolution theory has the challenge of lining them up in a tree diagram (cladogram) to tell the story of evolution. What specific problems can you imagine would happen when trying this? [173]

4. In the scenario above, the task seems impossible because it is based on the wrong assumption that all animals are related. Now think of the *creation orchard*, which is based on the idea that there were original kinds of animals that simply branched out as they expressed variety. How much simpler would that be? Why? [174]

5. How can the concept of a *creation orchard* help you minister to people who see the evidence for adaptation and variation, but mistake it for the type of evolution that can turn one kind of animal into another? [175]

6. Can you explain how each camp–evolution and creation–handles the fact that sometimes very distant animals share very similar structures? [176]

7. When we see similar traits specially tailored to each kind of animal, it speaks of design with a purpose. If God put that kind of forethought into engineering animals which aren't made in His image, what does it tell you about the special design He had for us? How does that make you feel? [177]

Lesson 6: Creation-Evolution 201: Fossils, Whales, and Extinction

 Watch the Video: *Fossils*

Videos available online: ***www.debunkevolution.com***

Fill-in-the Blanks: *Fossils*

Use the section below to fill in the blanks while watching the video:

Jane: Evolution predicts that we should have the fossils of the simplest creatures at the _____ [178] of the rock layers, showing a time when life supposedly started evolving on earth.

John: If evolution were true, we would expect to see single celled organisms down there. Then basic-looking multi-celled creatures above them. Instead we see Cambrian layers are full of very _____ [179] sea creatures with no clear ancestors in the lower rocks.

John: In Charles Darwin's book *On the Origin of Species*, he wrote, "Why, if species have descended from other species by insensibly fine gradations, do we not everywhere see innumerable _____ [180] forms?"

Jane: So in other words, most animals that have lived on the earth have been fossilized and _____ [181]?

John: Right. And if evolution was true, we should have millions of fossils that show us that evolution between all these animals since evolution is a
_____ [182] process.

Jane: Look right here. In both of these textbooks they show pictures of the *Archaeopteryx* fossil, supposedly
_____ [183] dinosaur and half bird.

John (reading): Alan Feduccia, a paleontologist who led studies in the origins of birds said this back in 1993, "Paleontologists have tried to turn *Archaeopteryx* into an earth-bound, feathered dinosaur. But it's not. It is a bird, a perching bird. And no amount of 'paleo babble' is going to _____ [184] that."

John: Wild pitches happen often in the game of evolution—like the fossil called *Tiktaalik*. It quickly became the missing link between fish and four-legged creatures that first _____ [185] on land.

John: But then in 2010 scientists announced in the journal, *Nature*, that they had found footprints of a four-legged land creature in Poland that are supposedly 10 million years older than *Tiktaalik*. So there goes *Tiktaalik* as a clear _____ [186] fossil. And yet, here it is, still in our textbook.

Jane: Evolution theory holds that Darwin's evolution tree started simple and then _____ [187] out to all the amazing animals we have today.

John: We see that there were many more
_____ [188] of animals than we have today.

Jane: And many of those went _____ [189]?

John: Opposite of _____ [190].

Jane: Wow! The idea that the fossil record shows a _____ [191] flood was a home run!

John: Yep. Fossil graveyards containing animals from land, sea, and air, all jumbled together. And in many cases the destruction was so powerful that fossilized creatures were ripped apart and buried quickly in mud. And 95% of the entire record is _____ [192] fossils buried mostly in land rocks, not ocean-bottom sediments!

John: So after 150 years, Darwin's theory was never proven true because when it comes to the fossil record, evolution _____ [193] out.

 Summary: *Fossils*

If evolution were true, the fossil record should clearly show it. But there are three major problems.

First, evolution predicts we should have fossils for the simplest organisms at the bottom of the fossil record, slowly increasing in complexity as we move upward. However, some of the lowest rock layers, called Cambrian, are filled with incredibly complicated creatures right at the start. For example, we find the trilobite, whose eye was more complex than ours, with many more lenses.

The second major problem is the lack of transitional fossils. Charles Darwin, in his book, *On the Origin of Species*, wrote, "Why, if species have descended from other species by insensibly fine gradations, do we not everywhere see innumerable transitional forms?" He thought future discoveries would find these fossils to prove his theory. For over 150 years we have been collecting fossils. We have over 200 million in

Most Animals Have Been Discovered in the Fossil Record!

Darwin hoped future fossils digs would reveal transitional forms. For more than 150 years, mankind has been collecting fossils. Of the 43 living land animal orders, such as carnivores, rodents, bats, and apes, nearly all, or 98% have been found as fossils. This means at least one example from each animal order has been collected as a fossil.

Of the 178 living land animal families, such as dogs, bears, hyenas, and cats, 88% have been found in fossils.

So in other words, most animals that have lived on the earth have been fossilized and discovered. If evolution were true, we should have millions of fossils to prove it!

museums, and we have found most of every type of animal that lived on earth. We should have millions of fossils that show an evolutionary transition, but while there are only a few that have been suggested, there really isn't one single transitional fossil.

Perhaps the best known was *Archaeopteryx*, which was supposed to be a transition between dinosaurs and birds. Alan Feduccia, a paleontologist who led studies in the origins of birds said this back in 1993, "Paleontologists have tried to turn Archaeopteryx into an earth-bound, feathered dinosaur. But it's not. It is a bird, a perching bird. And no amount of paleo babble' is going to change that." Since making that statement, there has been a constant battle in the evolutionary camp about whether *Archaeopteryx* should even be considered an ancestor to birds, and many are making the case that it should be thrown out of the evolutionary lineup. *Archaeopteryx* was even further disqualified as an evolutionary ancestor for birds when scientists found what appears to be a crow-size bird and extinct four-winged birds in rock layers designated to be below those containing *Archaeopteryx*.

Another popular "transitional fossil" was *Tiktaalik*, a supposed missing link between fish and land-dwelling animals. But then in 2010 scientists announced in the journal *Nature* that they had found footprints of a four-legged land creature in Poland that are supposedly 10 million years older than *Tiktaalik*. So it has also been removed from being a transition fossil. So to this day, no one has found the "in-between" fossils to prove Darwin right.

The third major problem for evolution is that we should see an *increase* of varieties of animals in the fossil record, but instead we see a record of extinction, which is the opposite of evolution.

In reality, the fossil record confirms a worldwide flood. There are fossil graveyards containing animals from land, sea, and air, all jumbled *together*. In many cases the destruction was so powerful that fossilized creatures were ripped apart and buried quickly in mud. And 95% of the entire record is marine fossils buried mostly in land rocks, not ocean-bottom sediments! Many of layers that contain fossils are so large that they stretch over many states, and sometimes cross continents.

So while evolution fails to explain the fossil record, the Biblical account of a worldwide flood does.

 Watch the Video: *Whale Evolution*

Videos available online: ***www.debunkevolution.com***

 Fill-in-the Blanks: *Whale Evolution*

John: Can you imagine what it'd take for a wolf-like creature to turn into a whale? The little tail would have to turn into a gigantic fluke, and the forelimbs would have to turn into _____[194].

Jane: They would need to evolve a brand new respiratory system. I mean, that's not easy. Then they would have to evolve a _____ [195] and their teeth would have to evolve into baleen.

Gameshow Host: It says, "Mesonychids are one hypothesized link between modern whales and certain _____ [196] animals."

Jane: What is the imagined category of animals that includes sheep, camels, pigs, cows, deer, and wolves—thought to be the possible ancestors of _____ [197]?

Gameshow Host: They only discovered partial fragments of the wolf-like skull. And since they didn't have the rest of the body, they imagined that it was an _____ [198] between a land animal and whale.

Gameshow Host: In your biology textbook it says, "The limb structure of this creature, called a ("walking whale") suggests that these animals could both swim in shallow water and walk on land." However, it appears to be nothing more than a _____ [199] animal.

Gameshow Host: This creature's often depicted in museums and textbooks with a tail fluke. However, they've never found the fossil bones for their _____ [200]!

Gameshow Host: This creature seems to be nothing more than an extinct _____ [201] creature.

Gameshow Host: This creature appears to be nothing more than an _____ [202] whale.

70

Gameshow Host: And the last two remaining names—Mysticeti and Odontoceti are just _____[203] whales.

Jane: And just like their whale chart, each of these animals was created by God to be _____[204] what it is.

 Summary: *Whale Evolution*

The theory of evolution holds that a 100-pound wolf-like creature became a 360,000 pound blue whale, but what would that really require? The little tail would have to turn into a gigantic fluke, and the forelimbs would have to turn into flippers. They would need to evolve a brand new respiratory system. Then they would have to evolve a blowhole and their teeth would have to evolve into baleen. Those are just some of the major changes; there are many more. Each textbook tells the story of whale evolution a little differently, but there are eight creatures that they often line-up to tell the story. The first is a theoretical ancestor from a group known as the Mesonychids. This classification includes such animals such as sheep, camels, pigs, cows, deer, and wolves.

The next creature in the line-up is Pakicetus. They only discovered partial fragments of the wolf-like skull. And since they didn't have the rest of the body, they imagined that it was an intermediate between a land animal and whale.

Next is Ambulocetus. It appears to be nothing more than a land animal. In other words, it was defined as a "walking whale," not because it had a whale's tail, or flippers, or a blowhole, but simply because they ***believed*** it to be. In fact, they didn't even find the part of the skull that would have a blowhole, but they still added a blowhole in museum drawings. And since it was a land animal with four legs, it was then called a "walking whale."

From there, Rodhocetus is often depicted in museums and textbooks with a tail fluke. However, they've never even found the fossil bones for their tail! Also, this creature was often portrayed with front flippers, until they found fossils to show it actually had front legs.

Basilosaurus seems to be nothing more than an extinct sea creature, and Dorudon appears to be an extinct whale. And the last two—Mysticetes and Odontocetes—are just modern whales.

So when a theoretical ancestor, a couple of extinct land animals, an extinct sea creature, an extinct whale, and two modern whales are all lined up, a story emerges that a 100-pound wolf-like creature turned into a

Junkyard Evolution

What if one day I decided to do a fossil dig at the junkyard? As I dig, I come across a bunch of cool stuff like bicycles, wagons, cars, etc. At the end of the day it hits me that these items have evolved from one another. To make my case, I begin to line them up:

First came the wheel itself. Next, it grew a seat and became a unicycle. Then a second tire, making it a little more stable. Then through an accident, a bicycle ended up with a third wheel, becoming a tricycle. Then four wheels become even more useful. Eventually a large change happened as it became a VW Bug. And that led to a beautiful red sports car.

When I line them up like that, I can make a convincing story that a wheel, over enough time, evolved into a sports car. But the truth is, each one was made fully formed with its specific purpose.

Likewise, various fossils can be lined up to tell an evolutionary story. But what if each creature was actually designed fully formed from the beginning for a specific purpose?

360,000-pound blue whale! But that doesn't mean that it's true!

Watch the Video: *Extinct Species*

Videos available online: ***www.debunkevolution.com***

 Fill-in-the Blanks: *Extinct Species*

Jane: Many evolutionists believe there were probably five different massive _____ [205] in earth's history.

John: So the most famous one is the huge _____, [206] right?

Jane: This theory's had some problems. First, some scientists dated the dinosaur extinction _____ [207] years after they say the asteroid hit.

Jane: Another study suggested that the asteroid was too wimpy to cause the mass extinction. Another team claims that they found dinosaur fossils that lived past the impact. So it's far from _____ [208].

Jane (reading): Right here it says, "Until recently researchers looked for a single cause for each mass extinction." Then it continues, "Many mass extinctions, however, were probably caused by several factors, working in combination: volcanic eruptions, moving _____ [209], and changing sea levels..."

Jane: But they just listed everything that would be taking place during the _____ [210] flood!

John: I've heard almost every dinosaur graveyard in the world shows fossils deposited by, or in watery mud or sand! And even more incredible, many dinosaur fossils

73

are found in a classic death _____ [211], with their necks arched back.

Jane: Evolutionists don't have a satisfactory explanation for one Ice Age, let alone 4 or 5. But the Flood gives enough calamity in a short enough time to actually make an Ice Age—there was only one—that happened a few _____ [212] years after the flood.

John: So when scientists try to stretch five extinctions, and five different ice ages over the evolutionary view of the geologic column, they're not sure how to explain why they happened. But when you compress the geologic column down into a Biblical time _____,[213] it's all explained by a worldwide flood followed by an ice age.

Summary: *Extinct Species*

Many evolutionists believe there were probably five different massive extinctions in earth's history. They date theses extinctions by where they believe they show up in the geologic column.

The first supposedly took place at the end of the Cretaceous Period. They believe this may have been the cause of the extinction of the dinosaurs and many other species. This theory's had some problems. First, some scientists date the dinosaur extinction 300,000 years after they asteroid hit. Another study suggested the asteroid was too wimpy to cause the mass extinction. Another team claims that they found dinosaur fossils that lived past the impact. So it's far from settled.

Benthonic foraminifera

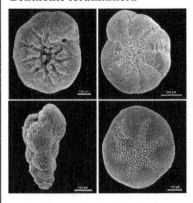

To better understand the past history of earth, scientists drill sea floor cores. Inside the cores are little fossils call Benthonic foraminifera. Researchers can compare the ratios of oxygen in these little creatures to estimate ocean temperatures at the time they were deposited in the sea floor.

Scientists have graphed the ocean temperatures over "millions of years." But do you know what happens if you shrink that data down into a Biblical Creation model of just 6,000 years? Right at the time of the worldwide flood, the oceans are much warmer! Then it gradually cools to what we have today.

This data fits the creationist model that after the flood, oceans were hotter, causing more evaporation, which causes global cooling! It seems to work with the idea that an ice age followed the flood.

As a matter of fact, there is no single theory about what caused these extinctions. The Miller and Levine *Biology* Textbook says, "Many mass extinctions, however, were probably caused by several factors, working in combination: volcanic eruptions, moving continents, and changing sea levels." It's interesting to note that all of these processes were probably working during the worldwide flood. This fits perfectly with all the massive fossil graveyards we find all around the world. For example, at the Lance Creek Formation in Wyoming, we find lots of species of dinosaurs mixed with birds, fish, crocodiles, lizards, snakes, turtles, frogs, salamanders, and small mammals—all laid down by a water catastrophe in sedimentary layers. Almost every dinosaur graveyard in the world shows fossils deposited by watery mud or sand! And even more incredible, many dinosaur fossils are found in a classic death pose, with their necks arched back.

Further, warmer oceans lead to more evaporation and cooler temperatures. Ash from volcanoes block radiation from the sun. Based on several studies and computer models, creationists believe these conditions during the flood would place the earth into an ice age. While many evolutionists believe in five ages (and don't have specific mechanisms for why they started), the evidence best seems to fit the idea that there was only one.

So when scientists try to stretch five extinctions, and five different ice ages over the evolutionary view of the geologic column, they're not sure how to explain why they happened. But when the geologic column is compressed into a Biblical time frame, it's all explained by a worldwide flood followed by an ice age.

 Biblical Discussion: *Fossils, Whale Evolution, & Extinct Species*

Discussion Questions:

Read Genesis 6:17

> *And behold, I Myself am bringing floodwaters on the earth, to destroy from under heaven all flesh in which is the breath of life; everything that is on the earth shall die.*

1. To create fossils, lots of water, mud, pressure, and the right chemical conditions are needed. How does Genesis 6:17 fulfill these conditions? [214]

2. What phrases can you find in this passage that indicates that it was a worldwide flood? [215]

Read Genesis 1:21

So God created great sea creatures and every living thing that moves, with which the waters abounded, according to their kind, and every winged bird according to its kind. And God saw that it was good.

3. How does this verse contrast to the evolutionary idea that a wolf-like creature evolved in a whale? [216]

Read Genesis 7:23

So He destroyed all living things which were on the face of the ground: both man and cattle, creeping thing and bird of the air. They were destroyed from the earth. Only Noah and those who were with him in the ark remained alive.

4. How does Genesis 7:23 explain the evidence they interpret as five different mass extinctions? [217]

5. Many people ridicule the flood account because they wonder how Noah could take care of all the sea creatures. How does this verse address this problem? [218]

6. This verse says that every air-breathing land creature that didn't go on the ark was destroyed. In your opinion, is that sufficient to create most of the fossil record at one time? [219]

7. In 1 Peter 3:18-22, God tells of another coming judgement. Can you explain how Noah and the ark are used in 2 Peter to demonstrate the coming judgement? [220]

Application: *Fossils, Whale Evolution, & Extinct Species*

The video presented evidence that the fossil record is in harmony with God's Word.

1. When we looked at the evolutionary story of a wolf-like creature turning into a whale, we saw that it was based on several theoretical ancestors, as opposed to actual fossils. Do you think the same applies to the "fish to land animal," "dinosaur to bird," and "ape to man" transitions, as well? [221]

2. How can you use the fossil record to encourage others in their faith? [222]

3. We see animals going extinct all the time, but no new kinds of animals being created. How could this be considered the opposite of evolution? [223]

4. How does extinction relate to the curse put on all Creation because of man's original rebellion? [224]

5. After going through this entire six-part series, what was your *favorite* apologetic? [225]

6. What has stood out to you the most? [226]

7. What has the Lord taught you through this series? [227]

Helpful Resources

The following websites are recommended for further research:

- Answers in Genesis: *www.answersingenesis.org*
- Answers in Genesis (High School Biology): *www.evolutionexposed.com*
- Creation Ministries International: *www.cmi.org*
- Creation Today: *www.creationtoday.org*
- Creation Wiki: *www.creationwiki.org*
- Evolution: The Grand Experiment with by Dr. Carl Werner: *www.thegrandexperiment.com*
- Institute for Creation Research: *www.icr.org*

Prayer of Salvation

You're not here by accident—God *loves* you and He *knows* who you are like no one else:

> *Lord, You have searched me and known me. You know my sitting down and my rising up; you understand my thought afar off. You comprehend my path and my lying down, and are acquainted with all my ways. For there is not a word on my tongue, but behold, O Lord, You know it altogether. You have hedged me behind and before, and laid Your hand upon me. Such knowledge is too wonderful for me; It is high, I cannot attain it. (Psalm 139:1–6)*

God loves you with an everlasting love, and with a love that can cover all of your transgressions—all that you have ever done wrong. But you have to *accept* His forgiveness. Your past is in the past. He wants to give you a new future, and new hope.

But starting this new journey requires a step—a step of faith. God has already reached out to you as far as He can. By giving His son to die for your sins on the Cross, He's done everything He can to reach out to you. The next step is yours to take, and this step requires praying in faith to receive His son into your heart. It also requires repentance for your past sins, and a surrendered heart that is willing to turn away from a sinful lifestyle. Don't worry about this part too much right now—for He loves you just as you are right now, and you'll have a much easier time leaving your sinful lifestyle after you receive Jesus into your heart. This is because the Holy Spirit enters your life when you receive Jesus, and He will lead you into a different lifestyle and way—a way that will lead to blessing, joy, and eternal life, but also a way that will be marked with tribulation, struggle, and persecution.

If you are ready to receive Him, let's quickly review some Biblical truths first.[b]

1. Acknowledge that your sin separates you from God. The Bible describes sin in many ways. Most simply, sin is our failure to measure up to God's holiness and His righteous standards. We sin by things we do, choices we make, attitudes we show, and thoughts we entertain. We also sin when we fail to do right things. The Bible also says that all people are sinners: "there is none righteous, not even one." No matter how good we try to be, none of us does right things all the time. The Bible is clear, "For all have sinned and come short of the glory of God" (Romans 3:23).

2. Our sins demand punishment—the punishment of death and separation from God. However, because of His great love, God sent His only Son Jesus to die for our sins: "God demonstrates His own love for us in this: While we were still sinners, Christ died for us" (Romans 5:8). For you to come to God you have to get rid of your sin problem. But, in our own strength, not one of us can do this! You can't make yourself right with God by being a better person. Only God can rescue us from our sins. He is willing to do this not because of anything you can offer Him, but **just because He loves you**! "He saved us, not because of righteous things we had done, but because of His mercy" (Titus 3:5).

3. It's only God's grace that allows you to come to Him—not your efforts to "clean up your life" or work your way to Heaven. You can't earn it. It's a free gift: "For it is by grace you have been saved, through faith—and this not from yourselves, it is the gift of God—not by works, so that no one can boast" (Ephesians 2:8–9).

---

[b] Summarized from: Southern Baptist Convention. "How to Become a Christian." *www.sbc.net/knowjesus/theplan.asp.* Accessed March 16, 2016.

4. For you to come to God, the penalty for your sin must be paid. God's gift to you is His son, Jesus, who paid the debt for you when He died on the Cross. "For the wages of sin is death, but the gift of God is eternal life in Jesus Christ our Lord" (Romans 6:23). God brought Jesus back from the dead. He provided the way for you to have a personal relationship with Him through Jesus.

When we realize how deeply our sin grieves the heart of God and how desperately we need a Savior, we are ready to receive God's offer of salvation. To admit we are sinners means turning away from our sin and selfishness and turning to follow Jesus. The Bible word for this is "repentance"—to change our thinking about how grievous sin is, so our thinking is in line with God's.

All that's left for you to do is to accept the gift that Jesus is holding out for you right now: "If you confess with your mouth, 'Jesus is Lord,' and believe in your heart that God raised him from the dead, you will be saved. For it is with your heart that you believe and are justified, and it is with your mouth that you confess and are saved" (Romans 10:9–10). God says that if you believe in His son, Jesus, you can live forever with Him in glory: "For God so loved the world that He gave his one and only Son, that whoever believes in him shall not perish, but have eternal life" (John 3:16).

Are you ready to accept the gift of eternal life that Jesus is offering you right now? Let's review what this commitment involves:

- I acknowledge I am a sinner in need of a Savior—this is to repent or turn away from sin.
- I believe in my heart that God raised Jesus from the dead—this is to trust that Jesus paid the full penalty for my sins.
- I confess Jesus as my Lord and my God—this is to surrender control of my life to Jesus.

- I receive Jesus as my Savior forever—this is to accept that God has done for me and in me what He promised.

If it is your sincere desire to receive Jesus into your heart as your personal Lord and Savior, then talk to God from your heart. Here's a suggested prayer:

> *"Lord Jesus, I know that I am a sinner and I do not deserve eternal life. But, I believe You died and rose from the grave to make me a new creation and to prepare me to dwell in your presence forever. Jesus, come into my life, take control of my life, forgive my sins and save me. I am now placing my trust in You alone for my salvation and I accept your free gift of eternal life."*

If you've prayed this prayer, it's important that you take these three next steps: First, go tell another Christian! Second, get plugged into a local church. Third, begin reading your Bible every day (we suggest starting with the book of John). Welcome to God's forever family!

Answer Key

Lesson 1: Why Does It Matter? (Fill-in-the Blanks)

1 - random
2 - chance
3 - Creator
4 - created
5 - destroyed
6 - cause
7 - life
8 - changes
9 - our
10 - death
11 - sin
12 - payment
13 - random
14 - existence
15 - ultimate
16 - purpose

Lesson 1: Why Does It Matter? (Biblical Discussion)

17 - This could have a figurative or literal meaning.
Figuratively, it could be that God calls judgement from heaven
and earth. Literally, it could mean that the heaven and the earth
are a testimony to the attributes and existence of God.
18 - This passage in Romans tells us that what may be known of
God has been shown to us through the things that are made, so
that we are without excuse.
19 - There are two basic reasons. First, evolution says that
millions of years of death is what created life. Secondly, people
have used evolutionary thinking as an excuse to murder others.
20 - Romans 6:23 says that death is the wage for sin.

21 - Open answer. Possible answers: confidence in God's Word, obeying God's Word, have a tool for witnessing, understanding God's authority, knowing that humans are made in God's image, etc.

22 - Open answer. Possible answers: However, it could include such answers as: disbelief, lack of confidence in God's Word, may lead to rejecting Christ, devaluing human life, misunderstanding of the truth, etc.

23 - Receive Christ's death on the cross, submit to Him and follow His ways, etc.

Lesson 1: Why Does It Matter? (Application)

24 - Open answer. Possible answers: Be their own moral authority, live without purpose, reject God's Word, devalue human life, elevate the creation instead of the Creator, etc.

25 - Open answer. Possible answers: Obey God, find and live the purpose He created for you, seek after His will, put others above yourself, live to serve Christ, etc.

26 - Open question. Possible answers: They compromise science, they compromise the Word of God, they have a lack of confidence in God's Word, they live ineffective lives, they begin to compromise other parts of Scripture, etc.

27 - Open question.

28 - Open question.

29 - Open question.

Lesson 2: Bible History: Real or Fiction? Radiometric Dating (Fill-in-the Blanks)

30 - refuted

31 - abandoned

32 - observation

33 - meteorites

34 - parent

35 - interpretation
36 - daughter
37 - contaminated
38 - rattled
39 - isotope
40 - removed
41 - constant
42 - 1954
43 - 1963
44 - 10
45 - 112
46 - undetectable

Lesson 2: Bible History: Real or Fiction? Uniformitarianism (Fill-in-the Blanks)

47 - Pangea
48 - continental
49 - sprint
50 - past
51 - catastrophic
52 - 200
53 - pliable
54 - missing
55 - minerals
56 - DNA
57 - Fossils

Lesson 2: Bible History: Real or Fiction? Radiometric Dating/Uniformitarianism (Biblical Discussion)

58 - Mankind wasn't there to observe when God created the earth. Instead of trusting in his own theories, we need to trust the Bible's chronologies to determine the age of the earth.
59 - God is showing that He is beyond our understanding. Instead of relying on man's fallible theories, we should trust the Genesis account of creation.

60 - "*all things continue as they were from the beginning of creation.*" Uniformitarian thinking says the processes we see operating today are the ones that have always been operating. It does not take into account catastrophes like the Worldwide Flood that could change things very rapidly.

61 - It means that God created by speaking His word. Psalm 33:9, "For He spoke, and it was *done;* He commanded, and it stood fast."

62 - That the world perished from a flood.

63 - No. It mentions the "earth" and the "world." It certainly doesn't appear that it is talking about a local flood.

64 - Scoffers

65 - That they purposely deny the creation and the worldwide flood.

66 - The return of the Messiah.

Lesson 2: Bible History: Real or Fiction? Radiometric Dating/Uniformitarianism (Application)

67 - It's because they have become convinced science has proven the earth to be old. They are trusting man's theories more than the plain meaning of the Scriptures.

68 - Not really. All of those dates are based mostly on radiometric dating.

69 - Uniformitarianism doesn't take into account past catastrophic events that could accomplish all of these things very rapidly.

70 - "Continental sprint" instead of "continental drift"; rapidly deposited layers; river systems quickly carved; layers bent while still soft; missing river delta at Grand Canyon; clams fossilized before it had a chance to open; a fish coming out of another's mouth; a marine reptile giving birth; dinosaur bones with red blood cells, soft tissue, protein, and DNA;

71 - 200 layers deposited in three hours; canyons carved through 700 feet of hard rock.

72 - Most people try to fit the millions of years into an imagined gap between verse 1 & 2 of Genesis, chapter 1; or try to stretch each day of creation to millions of years.

73 - Death is supposed to be the punishment for sin. However, if sin existed for millions of years before sin entered the world, then it couldn't be the wages of sin. (Romans 6:23; Romans 5:12).

Lesson 3: Human Evolution (Fill-in-the Blanks)

74 - evolution
75 - fake
76 - tooth
77 - extinct
78 - 40
79 - 10
80 - fiction
81 - already
82 - reclassified
83 - ape
84 - humans
85 - in-between
86 - pick-up
87 - truck

Lesson 3: Vestigial Structures (Fill-in-the Blanks)

88 - left-overs
89 - hip
90 - bones
91 - marine
92 - tails
93 - muscles
94 - worse
95 - throat

96 - good
97 - purpose

Lesson 3: Human Evolution/Vestigial Structures (Biblical Discussion)

98 - This verse distinguishes the difference between animals, like an ape, and humans. This is in harmony with the creation account in Genesis 1 in which we learn that all animals were created to reproduce "after their kind."
99 - Again, this verse is clearly saying that God created the animals separately, not a gradual progression.
100 - This verse shows that we were specially created, not slowly evolved from an ape-like creature.
101 - This verse shows that we were marvelously made, we aren't made from "left-overs."
102 - Evolution is supposed to be a process that takes place without intelligence. How could natural, random processes create such marvelous bodies that show amazing design?
103 - Open question. Here are some possible answers: They would have confidence in knowing they were created for a purpose, they would realize that they have a moral authority, they would know that God had a plan, etc.
104 - Again, it shows you that you have purpose, and that God had a specific reason for making you. It gives confidence in knowing that He will accomplish His plan for you.

Lesson 3: Human Evolution/Vestigial Structures (Application)

105 - Those who believe this say Adam and Eve were just a metaphor. It would take away the literal account of Adam and Eve—that God specially created them from the dust of the earth. It also erases the literal fall into sin, which ultimately affects the meaning of the cross.

106 - Open question, but here are some possible answers: Most people don't believe in evolution because they are personally convinced by the facts. Many believe because most scientists believe in evolution, or they are afraid of being considered stupid, or don't want to be accountable to God. Ultimately it comes down to what it says in Romans 1 that even though what may be known of God by what is made, they "suppress the truth in unrighteousness," and therefore "are without excuse."

107 - Not really. According to the Bible, humans were created in God's image, and animals are not. If we evolved from animals, how could we be made in God's image?

108 - Possible answers: Humans can communicate with God, separate from the animals, we have dominion over the animals, if we have accepted the gift of Christ's sacrifice on our behalf we will live eternally with God, humans can share many of God's attributes (fruit of the Spirit), and we can be redeemed through Christ's work on the cross. However, it is important to realize that man is currently living in a fallen world because of rebellion.

109 - It means that, as animals, that there is no absolute moral law, or law-giver. We decide all of our rules. It puts us in charge if there is no God and we are nothing more than animals.

110 - Possible answers: No purpose, believe they are the result of random-chance processes, no absolute morality, no eternal hope, believe humans are nothing more than animals.

111 - Open question, but here are some possible answers: You can encourage people that they have purpose, that they're not just the result of random evolutionary processes. You can show them that there is a literal Adam and Eve—and sin, and that they are in need of a literal Savior. You can demonstrate that if we are not animals, we are accountable to God. You can debunk the idea of evolution.

Lesson 4: Creation-Evolution 101: Adaptation (Fill-in-the Blanks)

112 - programmed
113 - recombination
114 - error
115 - code
116 - information
117 - blueprint
118 - varieties
119 - limits

Lesson 4: Natural Selection (Fill-in-the Blanks)

120 - survive
121 - observed
122 - complicated
123 - think
124 - random
125 - fit
126 - requires
127 - create
128 - simple
129 - death

Lesson 4: Adaptation/Natural Selection (Biblical Discussion)

130 - No. It seems like God is being very clear about telling us that each kind of animal was specially created.
131 - Again, the concept of *different* kinds of animals is mentioned several times throughout God's Word.
132 - Evolutionists often try to use the concept of *species* as a way of showing the evolutionary relationship of animals. Often if a creature expresses variety, it is named as a new species. Whereas the concept of *kind* is the idea of an original animal created by God. In other words, we may see several varieties of

dogs, but there was most likely only one created dog (wolf) kind.

133 - It should lead us to worship Christ for His creativity as Creator. Not only did He express His artistry in creating all the original kinds, but also designed all the variation that would be later expressed.

134 - At each stage of Creation Week, God saw His work as good. It was perfect, and un-touched by sin. Everything was created to accomplish the purpose He had for it.

135 - Christ died to take away the curse of death for those who have accepted his payment of death on the cross. Death no longer has power over the child of God because we will spend eternity with Him.

136 - Evolution sees death as the very creator of life. However, the Bible makes it clear that death is the punishment for man's rebellion (Romans 5:12, Romans 6:23) and has been conquered by Christ's death on the cross.

Lesson 4: Adaptation/Natural Selection (Application)

137 - Open question, but here are some possible answers: The literal account of Genesis and evolution are not compatible, evolution is bad science so it cannot even be considered, we shouldn't put man's theories over God's Word, etc.

138 - Adaptation and variation are observable, so we know that they are really happening. They are the result of genetic recombination expressed through the genetic variability that God packed into each kind. Mutations and natural selection have never been observed to create a new kind of creature. Mutations are a loss of information, and natural selection can only select from what already exists, so these two working together can never create anything.

139 - According to evolutionary theory mutations create a creature better equipped to survive, and natural selection kills-off the non-mutants. But in reality, mutants are almost always worse-off, and so natural selection weeds out the mutants— exactly the opposite of what evolution needs.
140 - Open question.
141 - Open question.
142 - Evolution is a religion of death. Christ's death on the cross conquered death and leads to life!
143 - Open question.

Lesson 5: Creation-Evolution 102: Common Ancestors/Branching (Fill-in-the Blanks)

144 - classification
145 - branched
146 - common
147 - relationships
148 - ancestor
149 - Darwin
150 - mutations
151 - morph
152 - 200
153 - Potential

Lesson 5: Creation-Evolution 102: Homologous Structures (Fill-in-the Blanks)

154 - common
155 - ancestor
156 - retina
157 - independent
158 - 4
159 - closely
160 - structure

161 - prove
162 - precisely
163 - circular

Lesson 5: Creation-Evolution 102: Common Ancestors/ Branching (Biblical Discussion)

164 - The creation account makes it clear that from the very start God created all living kinds of animals.
165 - Again, the orchard says that God started creation by creating kinds of animals, in this case, specific sea creatures and birds.
166 - God created fully formed whales from the very beginning.
167 - Genesis tells us that He made birds as their own kind right from the start.
168 - There is no one else who can create out of nothing. Imagine the power of God to speak all of creation into existence, it tells us that He alone is almighty. These attributes set Him up to be the one in charge, not man.
169 - Not only did God create, but He is the one upholding all things. Nothing can exist without Him.
170 - We should be moved to worship God for who He is. Creation testifies to His power and glory.

Lesson 5: Creation-Evolution 102: Common Ancestors/ Branching (Application)

171 - Possible answers: In the fossil record we see basic types of animals with variations, but never a transitional fossil from one kind to another. We see animals expressing adaptation and variation, but never has anyone observed one type of animal turning into another. In God's Word, God makes it clear that He created the animals separately, and to reproduce after their own kind—and yet we see the variety He has placed in each one.

172 - Here are some problems that might be encountered: gaps in similarities (in other words a missing transition between two types of animals), or two completely different animals on different "branches" that share one trait in common. Loops in which a trait appears for a while, and then disappears, only to appear again later. The most logical order may lead from a land animal to a sea creature, and then back to a land creature again. Some creatures would be so unique they don't even have a logical place in the line-up.

173 - Same as above, but with 8.7 million species, can you image the magnitude of problems they encounter?

174 - Instead of trying to place all 8.7 million species on a single tree to explain everything, think of how much easier it would be to recreate the *creation orchard*. Instead of operating on assumptions, creation scientists are using actual observable science. When animals can interbreed it demonstrates they are part of a created kind. While it is still a huge undertaking, using zoo records and other clues, creationists are working to map-out the *creation orchard*. This pursuit is called Baraminology—the study of God's original created kinds.

175 - Most Christians are confused because they see the clear evidence for adaptation and variation, but know they aren't supposed to believe in evolution. The *creation orchard* is a simple concept to help them understand that God created original kinds that expressed all kinds of variety – but with limits. It is a way of helping them merge observable science while staying true to the concept of "kinds" clearly stated in God's Word. For many it resolves a nagging problem and builds their faith.

176 - Evolutionists use similar structures in animals to make the case that they shared a common ancestor. Then they point to the fact that because they shared a common ancestor that is why they have similar traits – it is circular reasoning. But when two completely unrelated creatures share a trait, evolutionists claim that trait must have evolved twice. Creationists simply point out that similar traits are evidence they were made by the same Designer. Just like human designers use similar designs for different applications, like tires on airplanes, skateboards, cars, and motorcycles.

177 - Open question, possible answers would be: That we are made specifically in His image, that we are special. He gave us purpose. He lovingly designed us to accomplish His plan.

Lesson 6: Creation-Evolution 201: Fossils (Fill-in-the Blanks)

178 - bottom
179 - complex
180 - transitional
181 - discovered
182 - gradual
183 - half
184 - change
185 - walked
186 - transitional
187 - branched
188 - kinds
189 - extinct
190 - evolution
191 - worldwide
192 - marine
193 - strikes

Lesson 6: Creation-Evolution 201: Whale Evolution (Fill-in-the Blanks)

194 - flippers
195 - blowhole
196 - hoofed
197 - whales
198 - intermediate
199 - land
200 - tail
201 - sea
202 - extinct
203 - modern
204 - exactly

Lesson 6: Creation-Evolution 201: Extinct Species (Fill-in-the Blanks)

205 - extinctions
206 - asteroid
207 - 300,000
208 - settled
209 - continents
210 - worldwide
211 - pose
212 - hundred
213 - frame

Lesson 6: Creation-Evolution 201: Fossils, Whale Evolution, & Extinct Species (Biblical Discussion)

214 - Noah's flood killed all the land-welling, air breathing animals. Further, it provided all the water, mud, pressure, and chemicals (like silica from volcanoes) to fossilize many of the creatures caught in the flood.

98

215 - *floodwaters on **the earth**, to destroy **from under heaven all flesh**, **everything that is on the earth** shall die*

216 - While evolution teaches that there was a slow progression of several forms of animals from a wolf-like creature to a whale, this verse makes it clear that each animal was created as a fully formed kind from the very start.

217 - The textbook mentioned, "volcanic eruptions, moving continents, and changing sea levels" as being possible causes of the mass extinctions. Creationists have found great evidence that all of these were going on during the worldwide flood.

218 - Because it says, "all living things which were on the face of the ground: both man and cattle, creeping thing and bird of the air" were killed. That didn't include sea creatures.

219 - Yes. Creationists believe that most of the fossils were created during the time of the flood.

220 - The ark was what saved them from the worldwide flood, but Jesus will be the one to save from the coming judgement.

Lesson 6: Creation-Evolution 201: Fossils, Whale Evolution, & Extinct Species (Application)

221 - Yes. All of these supposed transitions are based on theoretical creatures, not actual fossils.

222 - Open question, but here is a possible answer: Many Christian believe that the fossil record proves evolution so they try to combine it with the Bible. You can use the fossil record to show them, instead, that the fossils prove the worldwide flood.

223 - Evolution assumes that new creatures should be evolving all the time. But we see the exact opposite, there are fewer and fewer kinds of animals.

224 - God created all things "very good." In Romans 5:12 it tells us that death entered through sin. Romans 8:20 tells us that the creation was cursed as a result of sin.

225 - Open question.

226 - Open question.

227 - Open question.

CPSIA information can be obtained
at www.ICGtesting.com
Printed in the USA
BVOW11s2236230916
462996BV00004B/7/P